# Why do they have to fight?

**REFUGEE CHILDREN'S STORIES from BOSNIA, KURDISTAN, SOMALIA and SRI LANKA**

the refugee council

Compiled by Jill Rutter,
Refugee Council
and Mano Candappa,
Institute of Education

## Acknowledgements

Most of the testimonies used in this book were collected during a research project about refugee children, funded by the Economic and Social Research Counci, project number L129251 009. The research project was carried out at the Thomas Coram Research Unit, Institute of Education, London University.

Thanks are extended to the children who allowed their testimonies to be used in the book. All of the testimonies are edited versions of complete interviews given to the researchers at the Thomas Coram Research Unit. A few personal details about the children have been altered to preserve anonymity. The schools who cooperated in the research project are also thanked.

The Refugee Council would like to thank the Commission of the European Communities Directorate General VIII for funding staff costs. Rohini Hensman for the use of 'Nathan', 'Krishna' and 'Vashti's' stories, Dina Mehmedbegovic, S. S. Ganeshanandan, Itohan Egharevba and Matthew Grenier for his editorial services.

Designed by Fiona Macintosh, Artloud
Printed by Typecast
Copyright Refugee Council, 1998

Cover photographs
Kurdish refugees, Diyabakir, Turkey. Howard Davies
Bosnian refugee mother and child, Croatia. They have just spent the night outside due to lack of accommodation. Howard Davies/UNHCR
Tamil refugee girl in India. UNHCR.

the refugee council

ISBN - 0 946787 18 2

Registered as the British Refugee Council under the Charities Act 1960 No 1014576
Registered Address 3 Bondway London SW8 1SJ

Refugee child's painting of a refugee camp in Sri Lanka

# Contents

Bosnian boy returning home

HOWARD DAVIES

## CHAPTER ONE
# Who Are Refugees?

In today's world there are nearly 14 million refugees. They are ordinary people, like Marella, Fatma, Baba and Nathan, whose stories are told in this book. They have fled from their country because of war, or because their religious or political beliefs or their ethnic group puts their lives in danger. The United Nations defines refugees as being people who have a 'well founded fear of being persecuted for reasons of race, religion, nationality, membership of a particular social group or political opinion.' (From the 1951 UN Convention Relating to the Status of Refugees)

Another 25 million more people have been displaced within their own countries, after being forced to leave their homes for the same reasons: fear of fighting, arrest or torture. Unlike refugees, internally displaced people remain in their own country.

One person in 150 is a refugee or displaced person in today's world, more than at any other time in history.

Refugee children at a London school          HOWARD DAVIES

There are refugees living in every country in the world, but today most refugees live in the poorer countries of Africa or Asia. In these countries, most refugees live in camps.  Refugee camps are no place to grow up. Children and their families may not have enough food and water.

The rich countries of Europe and North America have seen a rise in racism and nationalism. One aspect of this has been a change in the way that governments treat refugees. Since the mid-1980s it has become more difficult for refugees to reach safety in Europe. Refugees have also been made scapegoats by some politicians and the media. They have been blamed for causing social problems such as unemployment and homelessness. Public hostility to refugees has risen in many rich countries. This has included violent attacks on refugees and their homes.

The movement of refugees is one of the major political and moral issues facing today's world. It is important for tomorrow's voters to be aware why people become refugees and the support that they may need when they arrive in a new country.

# MARELLA'S STORY

Marella is Bosnian.
Marella and her family are now refugees in the UK.

"I was living in Bosnia near a town called Kljuc. When we had to leave we walked a really hard way through the woods. We walked and carried our stuff. We had blankets and we had clothes. We didn't have suitcases, we had bags like school bags. I had a brush to comb my hair and we had food. We couldn't walk on the road. There was a path through the woods where we walked. And then the Serbs found us. They took us somewhere that I don't know. They put an old man who fled with us on a cart. Then we were carried away, not on army trucks but in big lorries."

# FATMA'S STORY

Fatma is a Kurdish girl from Turkey who is now a refugee in the UK.

"In Turkey we weren't allowed to talk Kurdish, that was illegal. At home it was just whispering Kurdish. The police were always listening to our telephone and watching our flat. I don't know who you call them - the secret police I think, not uniformed police. They knew my Dad was always saying, "I'm Kurdish, not Turkish." Because of that my Dad got arrested. He was taken to a detention centre and beaten up."

# NATHAN'S STORY

**Nathan is a Sri Lankan Tamil. He left his mother and father behind when he fled from a village near Jaffna in Sri Lanka.**

"The Sri Lankan army was shelling and bombing from helicopters, near my house. So many people got killed, because they were shelling without looking here or there. One day when I went near the town I had a narrow escape, because a bomber plane was bombing. After this my mind was very upset. My father, my mother, everybody wanted me to go away, to leave the country, otherwise maybe I would be killed."

# BABA'S STORY

**Baba was 13 years old when he fled from Somalia.**

"When I was in Somalia all you can hear is guns. My dad, he's dead. In the first fighting in 1990 in Somalia, they killed him. Then in 1992 my brothers, my sisters, all of us, we took a bus to go to the market. We left my Mum in the house and when we came back she was not there. I need help to find my Mum. I came to London with my little brother and my uncle. Then after eight months my other brothers and sisters came."

# Refugees in Today's World

**Refugees in Europe**
About five million refugees are living in western European countries, from many different countries.

**Fighting and danger in Sudan**
There has been war in southern Sudan since the 1950s. Today the Sudanese government also imprisons those people who oppose it. The fighting and danger to those who oppose the government has caused over 400,000 people to flee as refugees. Another four million people have fled from their homes and moved to another part of Sudan.

**Refugees in West Africa**
War in Sierra Leone and Liberia has caused more than 1.75 million refugees to flee from their homes.

**In danger in Colombia**
Fighting in Colombia has caused over one million people to flee from their homes. Most of them have gone into hiding in other parts of the country. It is very difficult to get help to the refugees because many are hiding in the jungle.

Refugees have also fled from many other countries, including Algeria, Angola, Bangladesh, Bhutan, China (Tibet), Guatemala, India, Iraq, Iran, Kenya, Mali, Mauritania, Mozambique, Myanmar (Burma), Tajikistan, Togo, Vietnam, Western Sahara and Zaire.

**The war in the former Yugoslavia**
More than 3.5 million people fled from their homes between 1991 and 1995 during the fighting in Croatia and Bosnia. In 1998 fighting started again, between Serbs and Albanians in Kosova. Over 450,000 ethnic Albanians have been forced to flee as refugees.

**Kurdish Refugees**
Over 20 million Kurdish people live in the Middle East. In Turkey, Iran and Iraq, Kurds have been persecuted since the 1920s. Today there are over 400,000 Kurdish refugees in Europe and the Middle East and another 1,500,000 internally displaced people.

**Fighting in the Caucasus**
There are five wars being fought between different ethnic groups in southern Russia, Armenia, Azerbaijan and Georgia. Nearly 1,750,000 people have had to flee from their homes since 1990, and most of them have been unable to return home.

**The Palestinians: refugees for 50 years**
Over 4.25 million Palestinians are being helped by UNRWA, another United Nations organisation that works with Palestinian refugees. They fled their homes after Arab/Israeli wars in 1948/49 and in 1967.

**Afghan refugees**
There has been war in Afghanistan since 1979 and many refugees have fled from their homes. Although some refugees have been able to return home, over 2.6 million Afghan people are still refugees, living in camps in Iran and Pakistan.

**Going home to Eritrea**
The war in Eritrea ended in 1991. But fighting had destroyed houses, roads and schools and it was very difficult for refugees to return home. Now Eritrean refugees are starting to return home from the Sudan.

**The emergency in Rwanda and Burundi**
In Rwanda and Burundi there has been conflict between Hutu and Tutsi people for many years. In June 1994, after one million people, mostly Tutsi, were murdered, over two million Hutus fled as refugees to Zaire and other African countries. Over 870,500 people are still refugees.

**War in Somalia**
Refugees have been fleeing Somalia since 1988. In 1992, the Somali government collapsed and no political party was able to get enough support to form a new government. Since then there has been fighting between different groups in southern Somalia and 665,000 people have fled as refugees.

**Sri Lankan Tamil refugees**
Tamil people in Sri Lanka are an ethnic minority group. Some Tamils want an independent country and have been fighting for this. Ordinary people have been caught up in the war between Tamil fighters and the Sri Lankan army. Over 500,000 people are refugees in India, European countries and Canada. Many more people have fled their homes but are still in Sri Lanka.

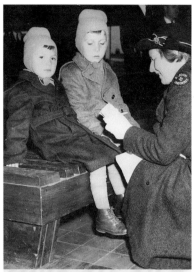
Polish refugee children arriving in the UK, 1946

# Refugees Throughout History

People have been force to flee as refugees throughout recorded history. Many religious books describe the stories of refugees who had to flee to safety. For example, the early history of the Jewish people contains many stories of refugees. The book of Exodus describes the escape of Jewish people from Egypt. Later, around 586 BC, the armies of Babylon attacked the area around Jerusalem and took 10,000 Jewish families into exile.

The infant Jesus, Mary and Joseph were forced to flee to Egypt, to escape the persecution of King Herod.

The Prophet Mohammed also had to flee from his home in Mecca. His religious beliefs put him and his followers in danger.

In more recent times, over three million Jewish people fled Russia, Poland and Romania, and settled in the USA, Canada, the UK, France and Germany. They fled violence and also extreme poverty, which often go hand in hand. During the Balkan Wars of 1912-13, Greeks, Turks and Bulgarians fled from their homes. The fighting of the First World War made over six million people refugees.

The Second World War left even more people homeless. In 1945 there were over 30 million refugees or displaced people, mostly living in terrible conditions in European countries. It was their experiences that made the newly-formed United Nations decide that there must be a better way of helping refugees. In 1946 the United Nations set up a new organisation called the International Refugee Organisation. In 1951 the International Refugee Organisation handed over its work to the United Nations High Commissioner for Refugees (UNHCR). At the same time the UN signed an international law to protect refugees. It was called the 1951 UN Convention Relating to the Status of Refugees.

During the 1950s and 1960s refugees continued to flee from their home countries. Most refugees at this time fled from human rights abuses in eastern Europe. In the 1970s increasing numbers of refugees fled from wars in the poor countries of Africa and Asia. Today the majority of the world's refugees live in neighbouring poor countries. But refugees are again fleeing war and human rights abuse, in Europe. The conflicts in the former Yugoslavia have caused nearly five million people to become refugees.

## Discussion Point

**Very few refugees are living in the UK, compared with many African and Asian countries. To some people, this means that the UK government and British people do not have a responsibility to help the world's refugees. Other people believe that all governments and people have a responsibility to help people in difficulty, such as refugees.**

**What do you think?**

# CHAPTER TWO

# Refugees from Bosnia

Between 1992 and 1995, fighting in Bosnia caused 3.7 million people to flee from their homes. A peace agreement was signed in 1995 that divided Bosnia into two parts: the Muslim Croat Federation and Republika Srbska. Although the fighting has stopped, many refugees are unable to return home because other people live in their homes.

About 9,000 Bosnian refugees now live in the UK. Here Marella and Fadil tell their stories.

A house damaged by shell fire, Sarajevo, Bosnia                UNHCR

## Bosnia

**Population** - 4.1 million
**Capital city** - Sarajevo
**Languages** - Serbo-Croat. In the Republika Srbska, Serbo-Croat is written using the Cyrillic script. In the Muslim-Croat Federation a Roman script is used and the language is usually called Bosnian.
**Ethnic and religious groups** - before the fighting about 40 per cent of the population of Bosnia were **Muslims**. Another 30 per cent of the population were **Serbs**. Most Serbs who are religious are Eastern Orthodox Christians. About 18 per cent of the population of Bosnia were **Croats**. Religious Croats are mostly Roman Catholic.
**Main exports** - Plums. The war has destroyed much of Bosnia's economy, but some small factories are now starting to operate again.

# ESCAPING TO SAFETY

Marella is Bosnian. She is now 11 years old. When she was six, her village was captured by the Bosnian Serb army and her father was taken to a Serbian concentration camp and treated very badly. Marella's father was then released and given permission to come to the UK. While this was happening Marella and other family members fled from Bosnia.

Today Marella lives in Essex with her parents and an older brother. Her grandmother lives nearby.

'I was living in Bosnia near a town called Kljuc. When we had to leave we walked a really hard way through the woods. We walked and carried our stuff. We had blankets and we had clothes. We didn't have suitcases, we had bags like school bags. I had a brush to comb my hair and we had food. We couldn't walk on the road. There was a path through the woods where we walked. And then the Serbs found us. They took us somewhere that I don't know. They put an old man who fled with us on a cart. Then we were carried away, not on army trucks but in big lorries.

We stayed in two towns. We went to one house and then we moved to another town and stayed there. And then we got away. The Serbs were not watching us as we were living in part of Serbia. We escaped to Germany by lorry.

My mum's family was in Germany. We stayed there for a little while and then we came to London. My dad was already in England. My dad sent a taxi to collect us in London.

My dad was waiting for us in our new home and my uncle and another uncle. I've got a photo of all of us which my dad took. I had not seen my dad for maybe over a year.'

# Bosnia: the past

**1900** The country that is now Bosnia was part of the Ottoman Empire at the beginning of the 20th century. To the north, Croatia and Slovenia were part of the Austro-Hungarian Empire.

**1918–1939** Yugoslavia - a new country - came into existence in December 1918, but from the start there was conflict between the many different ethnic groups who lived in Yugoslavia. In particular Croatian people fear the power of the Serbs.

**1939–1945** The conflict between Serbian and Croatian people gets worse during the Second World War. Nazi Germany invaded part of Yugoslavia in 1941. In Croatia, local supporters of the Nazis set up their own Nazi state. They murdered hundreds of thousands of Jews, Romany, Serbs, and Croatian opponents.

The Croatian Nazis are opposed by two groups of guerrillas. They are Josep Broz Tito's communists and the Serbian Chetniks. The Chetniks and communists also fight each other. Between

Bosnian refugee girls sheltering in Zagreb    UNHCR

organised street demonstrations. They wanted more rights. These demonstrations were put down by the army. Albanian teachers, doctors and civil servants are dismissed from their jobs and Albanian schools are closed. Slobodan Milosevic, a Serbian politician, claims that Kosovo will always be Serbian. He gained popularity among Serbs for his dealings with the Albanians.

**1941 and 1945** 1,700,000 people were killed in Yugoslavia, mostly by fellow Yugoslavs. The memories of the Second World War played a important part in fighting in Yugoslavia in the 1990s.

**1945** Josep Broz Tito's communists form the government of Yugoslavia. President Tito ruled from 1945 until his death in 1980. He tried to unite the population of Yugoslavia. He also created the largest army in Europe.

**1990** Yugoslavia remained a united country until the 1990s. But then Albanian people living in Kosovo

**1991** Croatia and Slovenia declare that they are independent countries. The Yugoslav army, controlled by Serbs, tried to stop them. After ten days of fighting in Slovenia, the country won its independence and the fighting moved on to Croatia. Thousands of people were killed and many more people, both Serb and Croat, become refugees.

**1992** Fighting in Croatia stopped after the UN brings in 14,000 peace-keeping soldiers. Fighting then started in Bosnia. Here Muslims make up 40 per cent of the population, Serbs 30 per cent and Croats 18 per cent. After the Bosnian

Parliament declared Bosnia to be an independent state, Bosnian Serbs decided they wanted their own country. Soon the army of the Bosnian Government is fighting the Bosnian Serb army.

**1992–1995** The war in Bosnia killed over 150,000 people. Many thousands of others were forced to leave their homes. Over 3.7 million people were refugees or internally displaced in Bosnia. The UN soldiers based in Bosnia are powerless to oppose the killing.

**1995** A peace agreement is signed in the USA. Fighting stops after Bosnia is divided into two separate areas. The Muslim-Croat Federation occupies 51 per cent of the country. The Republika Srbska occupies the rest of the land. Its population is mostly Serb. The European Community countries give money to help Bosnian refugees rebuild their homes.

**1997** Germany tried to send some Bosnian refugees back home. Other European countries opposed this move. Although some refugees are able to return, others cannot do so. They do not feel safe to return to land held by their former enemies.

13

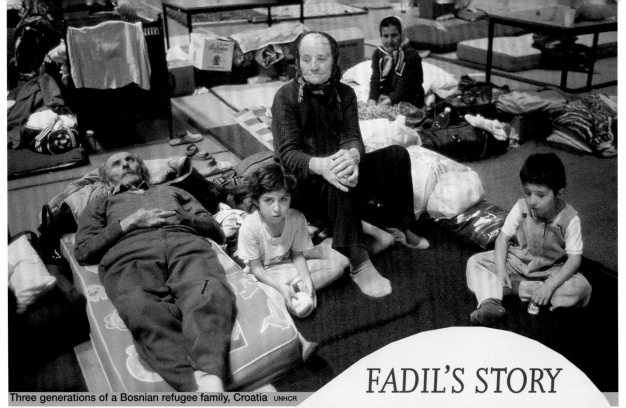

Three generations of a Bosnian refugee family, Croatia  UNHCR

# FADIL'S STORY

Fadil is a Bosnian Muslim boy. He was ten years old when he had to flee his home. Fadil's village had been captured by the Bosnian Serb army and his father had been taken prisoner. Like Marella, Fadil's father was later held in a Serbian concentration camp. While this was happening, Fadil, his mother, brother and sister fled to Croatia.

Fadil's father was later released and was brought to the UK. The rest of the family joined them later.

"In Bosnia we had a house, it was big and it was old. We were making a new house. Then the war started.

We went from Bosnia: my Mum, my sister, my brother and me. First we went to Croatia on lorries. There were lots of other people. We started in the morning about six o'clock and we were brought there about 12 o'clock at night. There was a hall where we were told to stay. We didn't have beds. I had a cover, quilt and a pillow. We had some milk.

After we arrived there was the Red Cross. We found out where the Red Cross was and they contacted my Dad.

We stayed in Croatia about two months, I think. Then we came to England by aeroplane. At the airport people were calling - a lady was calling our names. We had to go to a desk at the airport and my dad was waiting for us there. My dad took us home in a bus. I hadn't seen my dad for about year. There were lots of Bosnians that day at the airport. They all went to their dads.

My Dad, he can't do any work because he's got a bad back. And my mum, she doesn't do any work because she can't speak English. On my first day at school people spoke to me but I could not talk to them. I had a special teacher to help me. She used to take me out of lessons when she was teaching me English. At my school there are some kids who are nasty to Bosnians. They just swear at us when they saw us and they bullied us. Sometimes they hurt me."

# Organisations that work with refugees

Marella and Fadil and their families were helped by many different organisations. In Bosnia and Croatia, the United Nations High Commissioner for Refugees tried to see that they were safe and had some food. The Red Cross helped Fadil find his father. When they arrived in the UK Marella and Fadil's families were helped by the Refugee Council.

Throughout the world many different organisations are working to support refugees. Some are large but most are small. Some work in many different countries, others in just one country. The largest refugee organisation is the United Nations High Commissioner for Refugees - UNHCR

UNHCR was set up by the United Nations in 1951. Its headquarters are in Geneva, Switzerland and it has offices in more than 70 countries. UNHCR has three separate responsibilities:

◆ making sure that refugees are not sent back to places where their lives are in danger and seeing that governments treat refugees fairly;

◆ working with other organisations to make sure that aid reaches refugees;

◆ working for long-term solutions for refugees. UNHCR tries to help people return home if it becomes safe for them to do so. If this is impossible UNHCR helps people settle in a new country.

The British government gave £45 million to UNHCR in 1994.

Several other international organisations work with refugees. United Nations Relief and Works Agency for Palestine Refugees in the Near East (UNRWA) works with Palestinian refugees. The United Nations Children's Fund sometimes works with refugee children. The International Committee for the Red Cross often works in war zones with refugees and displaced people.

## Individual governments

Individual governments may work with refugee groups in their own countries. For example, the British government has paid for reception centres and help for 2,500 Bosnian refugees like Marella and Fadil who were given permission to stay in Britain for a limited period of time.

Arrival of UNHCR food aid and medical supplies for displaced people in Bosnia                    UNHCR

## Non-governmental organisations

Non-governmental organisations, known as NGOs, are not run by governments and are usually much smaller than international and government organisations. Usually they obtain their money from various sources including donations from members of the public.

Some non-governmental organisations work with refugees in poor countries. This group of organisations are sometimes know as overseas aid agencies. Oxfam and the Save the Children Fund are two examples of overseas aid agencies. They are working with all the major refugee groups in today's world, as well as many other poor people.

Overseas agencies do receive small amounts of money from governments but for most of their work they rely on donations from members of the public.

There are over 300 non-governmental organisations working with refugees in Britain. They include large charities like the Refugee Council, pressure groups and small self-help groups.

## The Refugee Council

The Refugee Council was set up in 1951. Today 160 staff and over 100 volunteers work in its offices.

## Self help

Throughout the world, in rich and poor countries, refugees are active in running support organisations to help themselves. There are about 280 refugee self-help groups in the UK, sometimes called

# THE REFUGEE COUNCIL

THE REFUGEE COUNCIL HELPS REFUGEES FROM MANY DIFFERENT COUNTRIES. ITS OFFICES ARE IN LONDON AND ABOUT 200 PEOPLE WORK AT THE REFUGEE COUNCIL

THE REFUGEE COUNCIL GIVES ADVICE TO REFUGEES. IT EXPLAINS TO THEM HOW THEY CAN FIND A HOUSE AND A SCHOOL FOR THEIR CHILDREN.

THE REFUGEE COUNCIL TRAINS REFUGEES SO THEY WILL FIND IT EASIER TO FIND WORK.

THE REFUGEE COUNCIL HAS JUST BUILT A HOME FOR REFUGEE CHILDREN WHO HAVE COME TO BRITAIN BY THEMSELVES. THE REFUGEE COUNCIL IS TAKING CARE OF ABOUT 20 REFUGEE CHILDREN WITHOUT PARENTS.

THE REFUGEE COUNCIL WRITES BOOKS AND LEAFLETS ABOUT REFUGEES. THESE BOOKS EXPLAIN ABOUT REFUGEES, AND HELP PEOPLE IN BRITAIN UNDERSTAND WHY PEOPLE LEAVE THEIR HOME COUNTRIES.

**refugee community organisations**.

Refugee self-help groups are usually small, often only employing one or two people. They may also use volunteer workers from their own communities.

Refugee self-help groups are an essential part of any work to support refugees. They help refugees gain control over their own lives. Refugee self-help groups are also places where refugees can meet other people from the home country and make new friends. For isolated refugees this is very important.

Self-help groups may organise a wide range of different

Bosnian refugee family resettled by the Refugee Council    HOWARD DAVIES

activities. They may offer **information and advice**, for example, or legal advice about staying in the UK. Refugee self-help groups may give help in finding housing and obtaining welfare payments. **Education and training** are important. Self-help groups may offer careers advice and language classes, or small-scale training for work.

Some refugees find it difficult to cope in a new country, because of past experiences or the huge changes in their lives. Many self-help groups offer **counselling** for refugees who have had terrible experiences or are finding it difficult to adapt to life in a new country. Counselling is usually given in the first language of a refugee and by someone who understands what it is like to flee from your homeland.

Some groups of refugees are more vulnerable such as the elderly or unaccompanied refugee children. Self-help groups may run activities for older people such as **lunch clubs** or **youth clubs** for unaccompanied refugee children.

Almost all refugee self-help groups organise **cultural**

Bosnian child learning her language at a community project in UK   HOWARD DAVIES

**activities** such as **religious celebrations** or musical performances. Bosnian groups celebrate *Bajram Kurban* (*Eid ul Adha* or the Feast of the Sacrifices).

Finally, refugee self-help groups work with young people. They run mother tongue schools for children so that they can maintain the language of their home country. There are now five Bosnian mother tongue schools in the UK. Marella and Fadil both go to a Bosnian language school on Saturday.

### Discussion point

What kind of help do refugees need when they first arrive in a new country? What kind of help do they need in the long-term?

Kurdish child's painting of police breaking up a demonstration in Turkey

# CHAPTER THREE

# Kurdish Refugees

There are over 20 million Kurdish people living in Armenia, Azerbaijan, Iran, Iraq, Lebanon, Syria and Turkey. The Kurds call the region they live in 'Kurdistan'. The Kurds are a distinct cultural group, different from their Turkish, Arab or Iranian neighbours. They have been a persecuted minority since the 19th century. Today there are about 400,000 Kurdish refugees in Europe and the Middle East and another 1,500,000 internally displaced people.

**Kurdish children, South East Turkey**  HOWARD DAVIES

## Where Kurdish people live

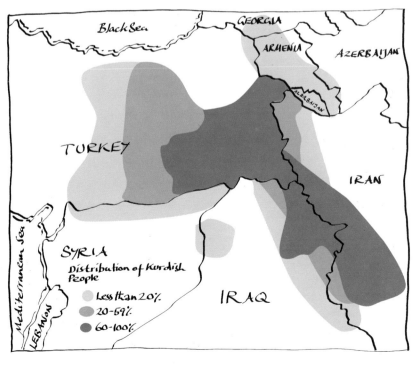

Black Sea

GEORGIA

ARMENIA

AZERBAIJAN

AZERBAIJAN

TURKEY

IRAN

Mediterranean Sea

SYRIA

Distribution of Kurdish People

⬤ Less than 20%
⬤ 20-59%
⬤ 60-100%

LEBANON

IRAQ

There are about 38,000 Kurdish refugees living in Britain. Most Kurdish refugees in Britain are from Turkey, although small numbers have fled from Iran and Iraq. Here Fatma, Metin and Serpil tell their stories.

# The Kurds: the past

## The Kurdish language

Most Kurds speak the Kurdish language - it is central to their identity as Kurds. The Kurdish language is most closely related to Persian. There are two main dialects of Kurdish. Kurdish

Kurdish refugees at a community centre, London HOWARD DAVIES

Kurmanji is written in Roman script and spoken in Turkey. Kurdish Sorani is written from right to left in Arabic script. Kurdish Sorani is spoken in Iraq and parts of Iran.

In Turkey it was forbidden to speak Kurdish from 1935 until 1991. It is now legal to speak Kurdish in Turkey, but the language cannot be used in political speeches or in newspapers. As a result very few Turkish Kurds can read or write Kurdish, although many are learning to do so in the UK. In Iran it was also forbidden to speak Kurdish for many years.

## THE KURDS: A PERSECUTED MINORITY

Fatma, a Kurdish girl from Turkey explains why her family fled as refugees.

"In Turkey we were not allowed to talk Kurdish, that was illegal. The police were always listening to our telephone, watching our flat. They were secret police, not in uniform. The secret police knew that my dad was always saying, "I'm Kurdish, not Turkish." Because of that my dad was arrested in Turkey and he was taken to a prison there and got beaten up. Now he has really bad back pains."

### Here you can learn to count in Kurdish

| English | | Kurdish Kurmanji | Kurdish Sorani | Sorani script | |
|---------|---|------------------|----------------|---------------|---|
| 1 | One | Yek | ١ | يه ك | Yak |
| 2 | Two | Didu | ٢ | دوو | Do |
| 3 | Three | Sise | ٣ | سێ | Se |
| 4 | Four | Car | ٤ | چوار | Chwar |
| 5 | Five | Penc | ٥ | پێنج | Penj |
| 6 | Six | Ses | ٦ | شەش | Shash |
| 7 | Seven | Heft | ٧ | ھەفت | Haft |
| 8 | Eight | Hest | ٨ | ھەشت | Hasht |
| 9 | Nine | Neh | ٩ | نۆ | No |
| 10 | Ten | Deh | ١٠ | دە | Da |

# The Kurds: the past

Archaeologists believe that Kurdish people have lived in the Middle East for at least 4,000 years. They have a distinct language and culture, different from their Turkish, Arab and Iranian neighbours.

## Turkey

Until the 20th century Turkey used to be the centre of the Ottoman Empire. In the early years of the 20th century, Kurdish people suffered at the hands of the new Turkish government. It denied that Kurds were an ethnic minority and some Kurdish villages were destroyed.

**1914–1918** During the First World War the Kurds helped the Allied Powers (UK, France and the USA) defeat the Ottoman Empire. The Kurds were promised their own country as a reward for their help.

**1918–1935** At the end of the First World War the Ottoman Empire was broken up. But the Kurds did not get their own country. Instead they found themselves divided and living in five different countries (Turkey, Iraq, Iran, Syria and the Soviet Union). In Turkey, Kurdish people continued to be treated badly. New laws were passed which forbade the use of the Kurdish language. All Kurdish schools and organisations were closed down.

The reaction of some Kurds was to rebel. In 1923 and 1927 Kurdish people demanded more rights. The Turkish government put down these rebellions very harshly and at least 100,000 Kurds were killed.

**1960–1998** The Kurds start to form their own political parties. All of them called for greater independence for Kurdish people. One political party, known as the PKK, uses violent means to fight for an independent Kurdistan. The Turkish government responded by arresting, torturing and killing Kurds who they suspect of supporting Kurdish political parties. Often the Turkish army enters villages and imprisons all the adult men, as a way of frightening the Kurdish people. Whole Kurdish villages have also been destroyed by the Turkish army and villagers forced to move to cities.

From 1980-1990 over 250,000 Kurdish people were tortured in prison. At least 15,000 Kurdish people were killed in eastern Turkey during this time. At the same time, the Turkish government failed to give economic help to eastern Turkey. The areas where the Kurds live are much poorer and unemployment is

Kurdish family enjoys a meal          MAGGIE LAMBERT

higher. Kurdish refugees from Turkey have fled to countries such as the UK, Germany and Sweden. Many of the refugees have been tortured in prison.

Kurdish refugees also live in **Iraq**. In 1988, some 80,000 Iraq Kurds fled to Turkey. They were escaping chemical weapons attacks by the Iraqi army. In 1991, at the end of the Gulf War 1,500,000 Iraqi Kurdish refugees fled to Turkey. They believed that the Iraqi army would use chemical weapons again. Almost all Iraqi Kurdish refugees have now returned home.

# ESCAPE! METIN'S STORY

**Metin was 11 years old when he escaped from Turkey.**

"I came to England by a lorry from Turkey, in February 1995, I think. From our house in Turkey we walked a bit, we got to a lorry - my mum, my two sisters and me. My mum told me that we were going to London, but I didn't believe her. In the lorry I was a bit scared. My mum wasn't saying anything. She looked a bit sad.

When we got to England they opened the lorry door, these men. They left us here. They dropped us and we waited some time, about half an hour and then our friends came."

# A NEW HOME AND A NEW SCHOOL

**Metin explains how it felt to start a new school.**

"When we came to England we stayed with out friends, all our family stayed in one room. We didn't go out that much and the room was very small. We were there for about a month, I think. I knew my mum didn't have any money for the things I wanted, so I didn't ask for anything. But I wanted some toys and games and other things.

I wanted to go to school, but my first day at school, I cried as I didn't want to be there. I didn't make any friends, nothing. I didn't understand anything and I didn't have any friends. I thought I would understand the teacher, but I didn't. My face was red, I think. After some time because I didn't understand any English, they took me to a special class."

# SERPIL STARTS SCHOOL

**Serpil is a Kurdish girl from Turkey.**

"Everybody kept staring at me. I was embarrassed and shy. Even at dinnertime I was scared to have my dinner. They were talking about me. I know they were talking about me because they were calling my name. I was really upset then.

I told my mum and dad and they told me when I get to learn English they wouldn't say anything to you. I kept crying and said to my dad, "I don't want to go to school, I don't want to see them laughing at me and see them talking about me."

I had two Turkish friends at school, but not that close. Sometimes they helped me, but most of the time they didn't. When they translated anything they were embarrassed. They were embarrassed that the other kids would say, "Don't talk to that girl, she doesn't speak English."

Teachers were always helping me with my work. There was a separate teacher who came to help me. I really like that teacher. I was happiest with her and not with the children in the class."

Kurdish boy, Mardin, Turkey    HOWARD DAVIES

# Refugees in the UK

Most of the world's refugees live in poor countries, but every year refugees also flee to the rich countries of Europe, North America and Australia. In 1997, 32,500 refugees and their families arrived in the UK.

In the UK refugees face a different set of challenges to those refugees living in the poorer countries of the world. In many parts of the rich world refugees have been made to feel unwelcome, by both governments and ordinary people.

Governments of rich countries have made it more difficult for refugees to enter their countries. Newly-arrived refugees have also lost their rights to permanent housing, work and college education in some countries. In the UK, newly-arrived refugees have no rights to permanent council housing. All newly-arrived refugees in the UK receive less benefits than do British citizens.

Governments argue that restricting the rights of newly-arrived refugees prevents people being tempted to move from their homes to come to rich countries. But cutting rights to housing, work and college education has made it more difficult for refugees to rebuild their lives.

## Bullying

Refugees have also been made scapegoats by some politicians and newspapers. They have been blamed for causing social problems such as unemployment and homelessness. Throughout the rich world the general public has become more hostile to refugees, without really understanding the dangers that caused them to flee. Refugee children even face hostility in schools. They often talk of being bullied, just because they are refugees and are seen as different.

Whatever your opinion, the movement of refugees and how they are treated in new countries is one of the biggest political issues facing today's world. We should be well informed on such an important issue.

# Refugees in the UK

| Country of origin | Main dates of entry | Numbers of refugees |
|---|---|---|
| Protestant refugees from the Spanish Netherlands and France | 1560-1700 | 150,000 |
| Jews from Poland, Russia, Austria and Romania | 1880-1914 | 200,000 |
| Belgians | 1914-1918 | 250,000 |
| Germany, Austria and Czechoslovakia | 1933-1939 | 56,000 |
| Basque refugee children | 1937 | 4,000 |
| Poland | 1939-1950 | 250,000 |
| Other European refugees from the Nazis | 1940-1945 | 100,000 |
| Czechoslovakia, Hungary and Romania | 1945-1950 | 50,000 |
| Hungary | 1956 | 17,000 |
| Czechoslovakia | 1968 | 5,000 |
| Uganda | 1972- | 37,000 |
| Chile | 1973-79 | 3,000 |
| Ethiopia and Eritrea | 1973- | 17,000 |
| Cyprus | 1974 | 24,000 |
| Vietnam | 1975-1992 | 24,000 |
| Iran | 1978- | 24,000 |
| Afghanistan | 1979- | 8,000 |
| Iraq | 1980 | 18,000 |
| Ghana | 1982-1996 | 17,000 |
| Sri Lanka (Tamils) | 1983- | 33,00 |
| Pakistan | 1984- | 6,000 |
| Somalia | 1988- | 100,000 |
| Turkey (Kurds) | 1989- | 30,000 |
| Congo (Zaire) | 1989- | 19,000 |
| Sudan | 1989- | 6,000 |
| Angola | 1990- | 12,000 |
| Bosnia | 1992-1996 | 9,000 |
| Sierra Leone | 1993- | 7,000 |
| Kenya | 1994- | 6,000 |
| Algeria | 1994- | 7,000 |
| Nigeria | 1994- | 8,000 |
| Yugoslavia (Kosova Albanians) | 1995- | 7,000 |
| Colombia | 1996- | 7,000 |

# Living with uncertainty and looking to the future

## FATMA TELLS OF HER HOPES AND FEARS

"When I first came here, I wanted to go home to Turkey. But after I understood what was going on at home and why we came, I was really pleased we came.

When we came here, we were allowed to stay for six months, then a year and then another six months. Then I think the Home Office gave us another six months after that as well. Then my dad was going to be deported - I was really sad about that. We had to go to court about this last month. Just before we went to court, we were sent a letter to say that my dad had to go back to Turkey. My dad was really shocked. He said, "This can't be, we've got to go to court in a few days time. What's wrong with them?"

It was me that sorted things out. I phoned up the Home Office, I argued with them, "How could you do this." My teacher was helping us quite a lot.

We are still waiting to hear from the court. They might let us stay for four years, and then after that they might give us proper forms. That is what I am hoping we will get. I am used to this country now.

If we went back to Turkey, we wouldn't be able to live. The Turkish police are searching for my dad. If they find him I am 99 per cent sure they will kill him and take my mum and sister away.

My mum and dad always tell me to make myself grow and achieve things. When we sit down and do nothing my mum and dad get angry. They say, "Oh child, there is so much you can do." My dad doesn't want us to get married young, because we see lots of people getting married young and getting into trouble. My dad says, "If you are older, over 25 or something, go ahead, no-one's there to stop you if you want to get married."

But I want to continue studying, I want to become an archaeologist."

## Dictionary

Being deported means being sent to live in another country, against your will. Sometimes people who have fled to the UK are not allowed to stay, and the government will decide to deport them, either to their home country or to another country.

## Discussion point

Why do you think the governments of rich countries, like the UK, have made it difficult for refugees to enter? What do you think of this?

Somali refugee family

HOWARD DAVIES

# CHAPTER FOUR

# Refugees from Somalia

There has been civil war in Somalia since 1983. Today nearly 665,000 Somalis are living as refugees, in Ethiopia, Kenya, Yemen and various European countries. Another 200,000 people are internally displaced in Somalia.

There are over 75,000 Somali refugees living in the UK. Here Sheikh, Basi, Kasim and Ragi tell their stories.

Somali refugee camp at the Kenyan border                    UNHCR

## Somalia and the Republic of Somaliland

**Population** - 7 million

**Capital City** - Mogadishu (Hargeysa is the capital of the unrecognised Republic of Somaliland).

**Languages** - Somali, Brava. Arabic is also widely understood.

**Ethnic groups** - Most people living in Somalia and the Republic of Somaliland are Somalis. Somali people also live in parts of Ethiopia, Djibouti and Kenya. Although most of the population belong to the same ethnic group, Somali society is now very divided. Somali society is divided into six clan families. Each clan family is divided into clans, branches and family groups. Somalis often give support to different political groups on the basis of the clan to which they belong.

An ethnic minority group called the Bravanese live in the coastal towns of southern Somalia. They speak a language called Brava at home, rather than Somali. Brava is a dialect of Swahili.

**Religion** - Most Somalis are Sunni Muslims.

**Main exports** - Most of Somalia is semi-desert apart from parts of southern Somalia where fruits and subsistence crops are grown. About 60 per cent of the population are nomadic farmers and make their living from grazing sheep, cattle and camels. Most of the animals are exported to Saudi Arabia, to provide food for pilgrims attending the Haj. Payments from Somalis working abroad are very important for the well-being of many Somali families. Today Somalis are working in the Gulf States and in Europe and sending money home.

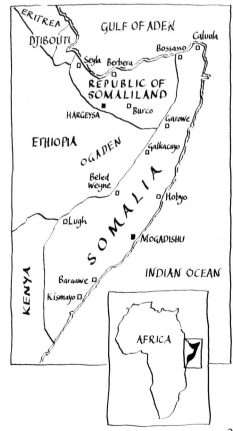

27

# THE CHAOS OF WAR

**Sheikh is a 14 year old boy who was born in Somalia. He has two older brothers and two sisters. When he was ten he and his family fled from Somalia to Kenya and lived there for two years, before Sheikh and his two sisters came to London. Sheikh is from an ethnic minority group in Somalia called the Bravanese.**

Sheikh explains what happened in the civil war and why his family had to leave Somalia.

"I was playing outside when some thugs came and told me, "Go and knock at your neighbours doors and speak Bravanese. Tell them to open the door or I am going to shoot you."  And then I went to knock.

I said, "Don't open it, there are some robbers here." But the thugs thought that I said, "Open the door." They didn't open the door. Then I said to the thugs, "They don't want to open it."

The robbers said, "Tell those people to open it." And I said to my neighbours, "Don't open the door because they are still here. They kill people."

The robbers said to me "You lied to us." They hit me with a gun. The gun never had any bullets so they just used it to hit my legs. Now I've a problem with my legs. They give me pain. When I came to London I had to go to hospital to get an operation.

One night some thieves came to break down my door. They were going to shoot my brother. My brother jumped on a thief and he went to call the police. All the time he was shouting 'robbers are breaking our door'.

The police came back to catch the thieves, but they came back to steal three times.

They wanted the gold and money. When they came in the morning the money was under the chair. I was at school and only my big sister was at home. They had a big gun and they told my sisters, "We are going to shoot you - where is the gold?" My sister said, "We haven't got any money." The robbers went in the bedrooms looking for money.

After the thieves kept coming we went to Kenya. We were scared."

# Somalia: the past

Archaeologists believe that Somali people have lived in East Africa for nearly 4,000 years. The ancient Egyptians called Somalia 'the Land of Punt' meaning the land of frankincense.

**900-1300 AD** Somali nomads and traders convert to Islam.

**19th century** The country that is now Somalia attracted the attention of European colonisers. By the end of the 19th century northern Somalia was a British colony, known as British Somaliland. The Italians ruled southern Somalia.

Somali sailors join the British navy. At the end of the 19th century some Somali sailors make their homes in London, Cardiff, Liverpool and other British ports.

**1899-1920** Sheikh Mohammed Abdilleh Hassan lead rebellions against the Ethiopians, Italians and British. Other Somalis join him in his call for an independent country.

**1941** Italian Somaliland was captured by the British army, with the help of its many Somali soldiers.

**1951-1960** Somalia was again divided, with the Italians returning to rule the south.

**1960** British and Italian Somaliland win their independence and are united to form one country.

**1969** The democratically elected Somali government lost public support. A group of army officers then seize power. Major-General Siad Barre became President.

**1972** The Somali language was written down for the first time. Students and school children go out to the country to teach people to read and write.

**1970-77** The Somali government was given increasing amounts of military aid by the Soviet Union. Somalia soon has one of the largest armies in Africa, despite being a very poor country.

**1977** The supply of weapons from the Soviet Union stopped as this country switches its support to the new Ethiopian government. The USA then started supplying weapons to Somalia. Neither the Soviet Union nor the USA gives much towards the economic development of Somalia. War then breaks out between Ethiopia and Somalia over control of the Ogaden region of Ethiopia.

**1983** There is growing opposition to the rule of President Siad Barre. Three opposition parties are formed and in 1983 they started to use violence to try and overthrow Siad Barre. The civil war in Somalia begins.

**1984** The fighting in northern Somalia was worst. Refugees fled to camps in Ethiopia. Conditions in the refugee camps were very bad.

**1988** The Somali government bombs the northern towns of Burao and Hargeysa. Over 400,000 people fled as refugees. Some refugees arrived in the UK, joining relatives who have lived there for many years.

**1990** Opposition to the rule of Siad Barre grows. There was more fighting. Many people who opposed the rule of Siad Barre are arrested, imprisoned or killed. Refugees start to flee from central and southern Somalia.

**1991** The United Somali Congress, an opposition group, took control of Mogadishu, the capital city. Siad Barre left the country. But the different political parties in Somalia cannot agree to form a new government. Soon they are fighting among themselves. They use the many weapons supplied by the Soviet Union and the USA. The fighting causes over one million people to flee from their homes.

very little fighting in the Republic of Somaliland. But there are food shortages in southern Somalia, as the fighting has stopped farmers from growing crops and selling them in markets.

**1992** Four million Somalis were at risk of starvation. But food aid is very difficult to deliver to southern Somalia because of the fighting. During 1992 about 500,000

**1993** UN peacekeeping soldiers take over from the US army, but armed robbery and fighting continued, mostly in Mogadishu and other towns in southern Somalia. Those fighting are often very young, some are only 12 years old.

**1995** UN troops left Somalia, although there is still heavy fighting in parts of the country. There is no government in southern Somalia. Large numbers of people are again threatened by food shortages.

Unloading food at a Somali refugee camp in Kenya — UNHCR

In 1991 the political groups that control northern Somalia declared independence. The new country is called the Republic of Somaliland. But it is not recognised by the UN, so it cannot get international aid to help it rebuild itself. By the end of 1991 there is

Somalis died of hunger, including half of all children under five. In December 1992 the US army lands in Somalia to help deliver food aid to starving people. This is successful, but the US army did not take weapons off those who are fighting.

**1997** Peace talks were held between the leaders of some of the armed groups in southern Somalia. Refugees continue to leave by land and sea. At the end of 1997 over 150,000 refugees were living in Kenya, 200,000 in Ethiopia, 45,000 in Yemen, 20,000 in Djibouti, and 150,000 in European countries.

# The arms trade

Most aid organisations believe that the military aid given to Somalia by the Soviet Union and the USA worsened poverty and conflict in that country, and caused more people to become refugees. These are arguments used against the trade in weapons. Not everyone agrees with them.

It is argued that poor countries spend money on their armed forces which could otherwise be spent on projects to help poor people. The money to buy one British Aerospace Hawk fighter jet could be used to provide clean drinking water to 1,500,000 people.

Buying weapons causes poor countries to go into debt. Throughout the 1970s many poor countries, including Somalia, borrowed money at low interest rates to be able to buy arms. In the 1980s interest rates went up and countries found they could not pay back their debts. Education and health projects were cut back in many poor countries that had large debts. This led to demonstrations and conflict.

Second hand weapons have also made wars worse in many poor countries. Since the end of communism in eastern Europe, governments throughout Europe have reduced the size of their armies. Many of their weapons have been sold - to poor countries. Today the wars in Afghanistan, Sierra Leone, Somalia and Sri Lanka are being fought with second hand weapons. These wars are all causing large numbers of refugees to flee.

Arms sales can also help governments that abuse human rights to hang on to power. These governments rely on powerful armies and police forces to keep their people in check. Soldiers and policemen have to be armed. The Turkish government is one kept in power by a large army. Many people have had to flee from Turkey as refugees.

Arms sales can also increase tensions between countries eventually leading to war. For example, the Iran/Iraq war of 1980-88 was partly caused by massive arms buying by both countries.

**Somali guerrillas with Russian and American weapons.** HAMISH WILSON

# THE FLIGHT TO SAFETY

**Sheikh tells of the difficult and dangerous boat journey to Kenya. Many Somali refugees have died making this journey.**

*"We took a ship from Somalia to Kenya. When we first went on the ship, it didn't move. Thieves came and they were shooting, they needed money. The thieves came with a boat. They were shooting guns and people were shouting. The captain of the ship was talking to them. He gave them something and they let us go.*

*All of my family were in the ship, all of my cousins and my Auntie. It took one week and it was very cold. I was scared. My Auntie was going crazy, she thought her baby would fall in the sea."*

# DEATH AT SEA

**Bazi is another Somali boy who fled from Somalia in a boat. Like Sheikh, he is Bravanese. Bazi has four brothers and one sister.**

*"We left by boat, but the boat broke down in the middle of the sea between Somalia and Kenya. One of our family fell in the water and drowned, it was our cousin. We prayed to God and He pushed us through the sea to the land.*

*The boat finally reached the sand on a small island. There was nobody there and for one day we slept on the sand. But we soon got scared. Some people then came in small boats. They came to collect us and they took us to their island. We were very hungry that day. They gave us food. We stayed there for a week. Then I was told that our family sent a small boat from Mombassa (Kenya) to that small island and they took us and we got to Kenya.*

*In Kenya we stayed in a refugee camp. There were bad diseases there. My grandma, she died of malaria."*

# Refugee camps

Bazi, like many other Somali refugees, lived in a refugee camp. Indeed, most refugees in African countries spend time in refugee camps. Aid organisations like UNHCR, that work in refugee camps, face many challenges in seeing that refugees have enough clean water, food and other basic needs.

## Water

Refugees who live in camps may not have access to sufficient clean water for drinking, cooking and washing. Ensuring that refugees have clean water is the first priority in an emergency situation. There are several different ways of providing clean water. If there are water-bearing rocks under a refugee camp, a well can be drilled. Alternatively water can be collected from a lake or river, purified and then brought by tanker to the camp.

## Food

Food aid has to be planned carefully. The food provided should not need too much cooking or too much firewood will be needed. (A lack of firewood is a major problem in refugee camps

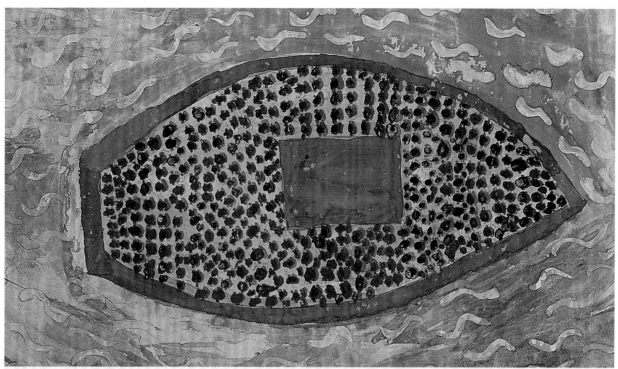

*Painting by Said Abdi Said (aged 14) of his journey by boat to Kenya.* **He says "I lived in Kismayo until the fighting became very bad. I left with my mother, brothers and sisters. We had to pay to go on this boat with many other people. It should have been fun, but the old peope were sick and we were leaving our home behind. For one day - OK, but two weeks!"**
From 'One Day We Had to Run", by Sybella Wilkes. Published by Evans Brothers. See 'Further Resources'.

and often trees around a refugee camp are quickly destroyed causing environmental damage). The food should be appropriate to local tastes and it should provide enough energy, protein, vitamins and minerals. Aid organisations also need to plan the transport of food aid. Refugee camps are often in isolated areas and food is a bulky product to transport.

## Planning

Refugees have many other needs that must be met. They will need shelter, particularly if they are living in an area where there is heavy rain or if it is cold at night. Medical care is also another need, as refugees may have war injuries, malnutrition or infectious diseases. Aid organisations also believe it is important that refugee children are given the opportunity to go to school as soon as possible, to give them a structure to their day and a sense of normality. Increasingly, in emergency situations aid organisations are providing basic materials for setting up a school - a blackboard and some books.

The delivery of emergency aid needs very careful planning and coordination. Many different organisations may work in a single refugee camp. They might include local health and education departments, UNHCR staff and those from other international organisations. Non-governmental organisations also work in refugee camps. It is important to ensure that work to assist refugees is well-coordinated. This is usually the responsibility of UNHCR.

# DIVIDED FAMILIES

Many refugee families are split up in their flight to safety. Here Kasim tells of his own family's experiences. Kasim is a 15 year old Somali boy who arrived in the UK three years ago with an aunt who was only a few years older than him. Kasim's mother is in Kenya.

"I came to this country in 1994. It was my birthday. I came with my aunt, who is my dad's sister. She brought me up. I've got two brothers, they are in Holland. My big sister, she's 17 this year and my two little sisters who are five and six, came to Britain later. My aunt looks after all of us. She takes my little sisters to school.

I am still worried about my mum. I can't do my homework. I can't do anything because I am so worried. When I walk down the street I think about my mum. Sometimes I cry, you know. Last week at school I was thinking about my mum and I was crying in my head. Then one boy hit me. I was so angry I got him back. That's how I almost got expelled.

My two brothers in Holland are eleven and nine. I think a family fostered them. I'm worried about them over there. Every night I worry. I'll try and bring all my family here when I am 18."

## Unaccompanied refugee children

The most needy of all refugees are unaccompanied refugee children like Ragi. These are refugee children who have become separated from their parents and have no other close relative who can care for them. Some unaccompanied refugee children get split up from their parents in the chaos of running away from fighting. Other refugee children are deliberately sent away by their parents, when it becomes too dangerous at home.

Today nearly 650,000 of the world's refugees are unaccompanied children. The largest group of unaccompanied children are from Rwanda. Over 100,000 Rwandan children became separated from their families in 1994 and 1995. In Europe, the largest group of unaccompanied refugee children are Albanian boys from Kosova in the Federal Republic of Yugoslavia. Their parents have sent them to safety in countries such as the UK and Germany, so that the boys are not forced to serve in the army. But every year unaccompanied refugee children from over 40 countries arrive in the UK.

### The right kind of help

Unaccompanied refugee children need food, clothing, shelter and care, like any other children. Most of the world's unaccompanied children are cared for in children's homes. But there are other ways of providing care. Organisations that work with refugees sometimes try and find foster parents for unaccompanied children.

Another way of helping older unaccompanied refugee children is to set up group homes. Here four or five children live together. They cook and do their own housework. Once or twice a week a social worker visits the group home to see if everyone is well.

Many unaccompanied refugee children need help in finding lost parents. Social workers from organisations like the Red Cross help unaccompanied children find their families. This task is called family tracing. The family tracer uses the skills that a detective would use, to look for lost family members. If an unaccompanied child's parents are found, that child can sometimes return home.

## Painful memories

But unaccompanied children need more that food, clothing and shelter. Many of them have hidden scars. They may have had terrifying experiences such as seeing a member of their family being killed. Other children may not know if their parents are alive or dead and may be very worried about them. All refugee children will miss relatives, friends, their toys and other familiar things.

They may need special help to overcome painful memories. Being able to talk about your problems to a social worker may be helpful. Other refugee children find that painting or writing helps them come to terms with painful memories.

Somali refugees arrive at Heathrow airport, London    HOWARD DAVIES

# UNACCOMPANIED REFUGEE CHILDREN

**Ragi is a Somali boy who arrived in Britain in 1995 when he was ten years old.**

"I came here by aeroplane from Africa, from Nairobi in Kenya. From the airport I came to London by train. A woman came with us. She took money from my family and she came with us. She had the passports and she did the talking. She answered when they asked questions at the airport. I don't know where she has gone now. Now I live with my uncle.

My mother, she is in Nairobi. My dad died in Somalia, in the first day of the fighting. He fell on the floor and the soldiers captured him. My mum told me he was killed. When he was dead we went to Kenya. My mum wanted to go. We went to Nairobi in 1991 and spent four or five years there. But in Nairobi the police come and they check all the people to see if they have got passports.

We left. Now I don't know how my mum is, or my brothers and sisters."

# ARTUR COREIRA

Artur Coreira, a young unaccompanied refugee lives
at a Refugee Council hostel for 16-18 year olds in London.

Artur remembers the fighting coming to his home town. Chaos broke out at school. When he returned home his house had been bombed and there was no trace of his parents or younger sister. He and his brother were helped to escape to the UK. On arrival he was lucky. He was taken to Korczak House, a children's home for unaccompanied refugees. He is now living in another home called the Cedars. This home prepares unaccompanied refugee children and young people for independent life. They learn how to cook, manage their money and other skills a person need to live alone.

Artur is studying at a local college. He also plays football for Wimbledon Under 18s and looks set for a career as a professional footballer. This is what Artur has to say:

*"We were frightened when we got to England. But we were taken to Korczak House and I loved it there. I felt protected. I couldn't speak any English when I first came. I used to get bullied at school. But I worked very hard and passed my examinations. I am now studying French and Spanish at college. The Cedars is a good place to live because of the staff and the atmosphere. I like my bedroom, its like having my own house. I feel more in control of my life there. We do our own cooking and cleaning.*

*I've always loved sport. I played a short time for West Ham and since July I've been playing for Wimbledon. Playing football has been my dream since I've been very young.*

*Life is still difficult at times, especially when I think of my family. But I just think to myself that I have to be strong. I don't want to waste my time here. I love my family and if they are still alive I want to concentrate my life to help them. I'd like to go back to Angola one day. But England would definitely be my second home."*

## Discussion point

Over 625,000 jobs depend on manufacturing weapons in the UK. But should we sell arms to countries that are fighting wars or to governments that abuse human rights?
**What do you think?**

# CHAPTER FIVE

# Tamil Refugees from Sri Lanka

Tamil child's painting of bombing by Sri Lankan air force near Jaffna

A civil war between Tamil fighters and the Sri Lankan government has caused over 500,000 refugees to flee to India, Europe and North America. Another 900,000 people are internally displaced in Sri Lanka.

There are over 35,000 Tamil refugees living in the UK. Here Krishna, Vashti, Arjun, Rasan, Radhika and Lakshmi tell their stories.

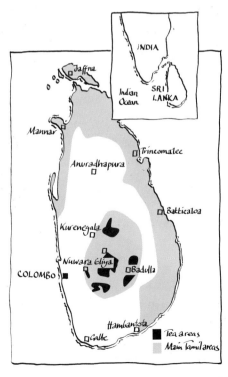

## Sri Lanka

**Population** - 17 million
**Capital city** - Colombo
**Languages** - Sinhala, Tamil and English
**Ethnic groups** - Some 74 per cent of the population are Sinhalese. Another 18 per cent of people are Tamils. Sri Lankan Muslims form another 7 per cent of the population. They are known as Moors and speak Tamil as their first language. There are also a small number of indigenous people and the descendants of Dutch and Portuguese settlers.
**Religion** - Most Sinhalese people are Buddhists. Tamil people are mostly Hindu. There are also smaller numbers of Muslims and Christians.
**Main exports** - Tea is the main export and is grown on tea plantations in central Sri Lanka. The economy has been badly affected by the war.

# FLIGHT
# KRISHNA'S STORY

**Krishna is a Sri Lankan Tamil. He and his family lived in Colombo until they had to flee in 1983.**

"I was in the eighth grade at school in Colombo. I was actually at school when my grandmother came and got me at mid-day because troubles were breaking out on the street - that's how it all started. Then we went to Jaffna where there wasn't any trouble at that time. We had Indian ships coming to take us there. I studied in Jaffna for one year, finishing my eighth grade. I started my ninth grade but then the army started bombing from the sea. We had to go to our granddad's house through all these lanes and jumping over fences because the army was coming.

So we - all the family - went to Colombo again because at this time it was Jaffna that was unsafe. I went to another school again and tried to finish the ninth grade. Then we came to Britain. It was very sudden."

# ESCAPING
# THE GUERRILLAS

**Vashti is a Tamil girl who lived in Jaffna. She came to London with her parents and younger brother.**

"I was studying hard at school because I really wanted to enter the university, but you couldn't study peacefully. All the time there was something going on and the situation was getting worse and worse. Then the Tigers (guerrillas) and others were coming and pushing us to join them. They just came into the school. Our principal was really strict and she wouldn't allow us to go and join. So later on the Tigers got admission at gun-point, so the principal couldn't do anything. They just came in and said, 'sign this form' and all that. Some girls joined and a couple of them died in the fighting, I heard later on.

My parents took that really seriously, you know, they were scared for me and my brother. He's really small now, but when he grows up he might get into that sort of thing."

# Sri Lanka: the past

In the 5th century BC, ancestors of Tamil and Sinhalese people arrived in Sri Lanka after migrating from southern India. By the time Portuguese explorers arrived in 1505, there were three kingdoms on the island. There was a Tamil kingdom in northern Sri Lanka and two Sinhalese kingdoms in the south. The Portuguese named the island Ceylon.

**1656** Dutch colonists captured most of Ceylon from the Portuguese. The Dutch took much farm land to grow coffee, sugar cane, spices and tobacco.

**1796** The Dutch signed an agreement with a trading company called the British East India Company. Ceylon is handed over to the British East India Company which made large profits from coffee, spices and sugar.

**1840** The British passed a law which allowed them to claim any land where the farmer cannot prove ownership. Since many farmers did not have legal documents, this allowed the British to claim many farms. The land was then sold on very cheaply to British plantation owners. Coffee and rubber are grown on the plantations. Indian Tamils are brought to work on the coffee plantations of central Ceylon.

**1870** Coffee bushes were killed by a fungal disease. Tea is planted in their place and it became Ceylon's main export.

**1948** Ceylon gains independence from the British. One of the first acts of the new government is to make plantation Tamils stateless. They also lose their right to vote.

**1956** Sinhala became Sri Lanka's official language, replacing English as the language of government. Many Tamil civil servants were worried that they will lose their jobs as their Sinhala was not good enough. There was a demonstration about the change in official language by Tamil MPs. The peaceful demonstration turned into a riot after Sinhalese racists stone the demonstration. Over 150 Tamils were killed.

**1958** Sinhalese racists attacked Tamils, killing over 1,000 people. British and French ships have to rescue 12,000 Tamil refugees from Colombo.

**1972** Ceylon was renamed Sri Lanka and Buddhism was made the state religion.

**1976** Tamil leaders met and call for a separate state for Tamil people. Most Sri Lankan Tamils supported this plan, as they felt they had no rights in Sri Lanka. At the same time a group of young Tamils founded an organisation called the Liberation Tigers of Tamil Eelam. This organisation uses violent means to fight for an independent Tamil state.

**1977** Over 500 Tamil people were killed in anti-Tamil violence.

**1983** Violence against Tamil people worsened. In July 1983 a week of riots left 2,000 people dead and caused 150,000 Tamils to flee as refugees. Over 23,000 businesses and homes were destroyed, mostly in Colombo.

**Tamil refugee girl with her identity documents**          HOWARD DAVIES

Tamil refugees flee to India, Europe and North America.

**1985** The fighting between the Sri Lankan army and Tamil guerrillas grew worse. The Indian government arranged peace talks between the Sri Lankan government, Tamil political parties and Tamil guerrillas. The peace talks, however, were not successful.

**1987** The Indian government sent soldiers to Sri Lanka, to try and keep peace. Indian soldiers, however, were soon accused of killing innocent people by human rights organisations like Amnesty International.

**1990** Fighting continued in northern Sri Lanka. The Sri Lankan army stopped food, medicine and other essential goods from entering the Tamil town of Jaffna. Here there is no electricity and people have very little to eat.

**1994** Elections in Sri Lanka brought a new government to power. There was a break in the fighting and peace talks were arranged.

**1995 – 1998** Fighting started again. By 1998, over 515,000 Sri Lankans were refugees and another 900,000 people internally displaced.

# Refugees

Some 515,000 Sri Lankans are refugees, mostly in India, Europe and North America. Another 900,000 Sri Lankan people are internally displaced. They have fled fighting. But there are other dangers facing Tamil people. Young Tamil men may be arrested by the Sri Lankan police and army and accused of supporting Tamil guerrillas. Hundreds of young Tamils have disappeared after arrest. Young Tamils may also be forced to join Tamil guerrillas. Some might be forced into suicide missions.

Internally displaced people living in Sri Lanka are very vulnerable. Some of them are in hiding in the forests, without food, shelter and clean drinking water. It is very difficult to get aid to these people. Other internally displaced people are living in camps. Here they are being given some food, but lack other very basic needs such as medicine and milk for children. A recent survey showed that 71 per cent of Tamil children living in refugee camps suffered from malnutrition.

Over 70,000 Tamil refugees live in camps in south India.

Tamil woman, northern Sri Lanka. She has been helped to return to her home after being a refugee in India

UNHCR

Another 100,000 Tamil refugees live outside refugee camps, in cities such as Madras. Here they depend on money sent back by relatives living abroad.

Tamil refugees have also fled to Europe and North America. The refugees have often had to pay criminals large sums of money to arrange flights and false passports and visas.

Life has not been easy for Tamil refugees in Europe. Many European countries have refused to believe the stories of persecution that Tamil refugees told. Many Tamil refugees are denied permission to remain in Europe. In 1995 Norway and Switzerland announced that they were going to be returning large numbers of Tamil refugees to Colombo.

## Sri Lankan Asylum-seekers and Refugees

| | |
|---|---|
| India | 170,000 |
| Germany | 60,000 |
| France | 40,000 |
| Netherlands | 15,000 |
| UK | 35,000 |
| Switzerland | 40,000 |
| Other European countries | 15,000 |
| USA | 15,000 |
| Canada | 125,000 |

# THE LONG JOURNEY TO SAFETY

Arjun is a Tamil boy from Sri Lanka. At the age of six years Arjun and his mother and sisters fled from his home in Jaffna to escape fighting. It took the family three years to reach London and be reunited with Arjun's father who had left Sri Lanka before them. Like many refugees, Arjun's family had to pay money to agents to arrange their escape.

"We drove from Jaffna to Colombo by car and then took a plane to Singapore. We arrived in Singapore and stayed there for one week. It wasn't only us, there were plenty of people. They wanted to go to Germany and all different countries. They were all living in our hotel.

We stayed in our hotel for one week. The agents arranged all that. My dad gave money to them. And they gave us food and stuff.

And then we arrived in Bombay. From there I think it was Africa. And we stayed for two years because we had all these problems with passports and everything. The agents were messing us around and they lied to us, so we stayed there for two years. We stayed in a big house and we had to cook. We had no money and sometimes my dad sent money to us.

Two men died there. They got sick with malaria, many people get sick there. All sorts of people came to the house, Sri Lankans to go to Germany, to Britain, to France and other places. Mum was angry with the agents because we were going to come to Britain straight away from Colombo, but the agents made us stay in Africa for a long time.

There were six or seven rooms upstairs and downstairs in the house. Downstairs it was a big place and we could play there. I got to know some children because I stayed for two years and I got some friends. But I couldn't go to school.

Then I came to Holland and from Holland I came to Germany, Germany to France and its a long story! This was all because of the agents as well. We spent a lot of money because of the agents.

I stayed in Germany for six months. We stayed with Auntie which was nice. From Germany I went to France in my uncle's car. Then we stayed in my uncle's house in France for about a week. We left France in my uncle's car and went to Dover. I didn't have a passport of my own, so I had to dress up as a girl! I had to dress up as a girl so when they asked for a passport we showed a girl's passport and we came through. I was wearing a hat. My sisters, they were laughing at me.

My dad was in Britain, so that's why we came to Britain you see. He was over here before us and had lived in England for about six years.

We arrived in the morning about six. It was a Sunday. My dad, he was at home. He was different from before. He was very different and felt like a stranger to me.

It took two or three years to reach England. That is why I was late starting my education. It was hard on me at school. I was in Year Two in Jaffna and I was in Year Five in London.

I don't think about all of this anymore, but if I do, it's really strange and horrible."

# LAKSHMI'S HOPES FOR THE FUTURE

Lakshmi is a 12 year old Sri Lankan Tamil girl who left Colombo with her parents and sister when she was seven. She misses her family in Sri Lanka badly.

"I don't know why they have to fight in our country, but I feel sorry for the people in Sri Lanka. Most of all I pray for our family, my Dad's family and my Mum's family.

The difficulty for me is that I don't exactly understand what is going on. Why do they have to fight? It is unfair for the innocent people.

I hope that the fighting stops soon and that everyone can have a normal life and that children get the chance to go to school."

Tamil child at a mother tongue school in London
HOWARD DAVIES

# RADHIKA'S JOURNEY

Radhika fled from Jaffna to Colombo with her family when she was seven. They lived safely in Colombo for five years, but then had to leave when anti-Tamil riots started there. Like Arjun, Radhika's family had to pay agents to arrange their escape.

"The Tigers asked my brother to join them. My Mum didn't let him and we had to leave. We came to the water and had to pay money to the army to let us leave. Mum was holding me. Mum told the army she didn't have any money. She said, "Look at my children, I don't have any money, I have many girls and I don't have any money."

"We stayed in Colombo about five years. We bought a small house, only one room with a kitchen and a bathroom. We were studying there. Our best friends were there. And then the fighting started. The fighting was round the corner.

We left Colombo and we went to Moscow. We stayed there for two days and then we went to Nigeria. We stayed there for one week or two weeks. Agents were helping us. In Moscow it was all snow. In Nigeria it was really hot.

In Nigeria there was a Tamil man. He took us to a flat to stay for one week. We just ate bread. Then we went to another place, there were all Tamil and Muslim people living there, one room for one family. We all cooked together in the kitchen, food like rice and curry.

When we came to London we didn't know where we were going to live, or if we would stay or go back. They might still send us back."

# Refugee children's education

For refugees, both adults and children, education is often the route to rebuilding their lives in a new country. But many refugee children do not go to school. Only 12 per cent of the world's refugee children are presently receiving an education. Organisations like the UNHCR are now working to ensure that more refugee children will be able to go to school.

The UNHCR feels that refugee children can go to school as soon as possible after leaving their home country - even if this means a school under a tree in a refugee camp. For children who have fled fighting, a school can give a child an sense of stability and security, and the chance to make new friends.

## The benefits of schooling

Among teenagers, particularly boys, the chance to go to school can take the pressure away from being a child soldier. In countries such as Afghanistan, Angola, Liberia, Mali, Sierra Leone, Somalia, Sri Lanka and Sudan, children

as young as ten may be encouraged to fight. Education can offer an alternative future to that of being a child soldier.

Schools can also deliver messages important to the survival of newly-arrived refugees. In refugee camps, schools have been used to deliver messages about health care, family tracing and land mine awareness. For example, schools in Rwandan refugee camps in Tanzania were used to deliver messages about the prevention of diseases.

Schools can free mothers of child care responsibilities, enabling them to work. This may be important in refugee camps where there are large number of single mothers, - because their men might have been killed in fighting.

In the long term schools can be used to try and solve the conflicts that cause people to become refugees. Dance, drama, music, sport and discussion can be used to bring young people of different ethnic groups together, and to break down hatreds that cause wars. In Sri Lanka there are many small organisations working with young Sinhalese and Tamils (including internally

displaced people) to break down the hatreds that caused the conflict.

## Practical issues

In camps in Africa and Asia refugees have often been able to set up schools soon after arriving in a new country, often with the minimum of resources. Refugees who were teachers in their home country often take the lead in doing this. To help refugee teachers do this, aid organisations such as the UNICEF - the United Nations Children's Fund - have been providing 'the school in a box' to volunteer refugee teachers. The school in a box contains the basic equipment needed to set up a school, such as slates, chalk, a blackboard, exercise books and some text books.

In Australasia, Europe and North America, refugee children usually attend the same schools as any other child. Here refugee children face a different set of challenges. They have to learn a new language very quickly. Sometimes, the memories of what happened at home can make it difficult to concentrate on lessons. Sadly, refugee children sometimes face bullying in new schools. But given sympathy and help, refugee children are often very successful in their new schools.

## Mother tongue schools

At weekends and evenings refugee children can be found learning their first language in living rooms, halls and empty school buildings. They are students in mother tongue schools, run by refugees themselves.

Going to school on Saturday may seem like a bad idea, but there are many benefits for refugee children. It is always useful to know two languages rather than one. Mother tongue schools enable refugee children to meet others from a similar background, and to talk about things that are important in their lives. For refugee children knowing how to read and write your first language is important, if one day, you might wish to return to your home country.

The teachers in mother tongue schools are usually volunteers. Parents may help run the school, helping in class and in sports and cultural events.

There are mother tongue schools in most countries which have a large refugee

Tamil child at a mother tongue school in London
HOWARD DAVIES

populations. In Britain three are over 20 Tamil mother tongue schools. In Denmark, Finland, Norway and Sweden, refugee children are allowed to learn their first language during school time, rather than at weekends. The governments in these countries pay for refugee children to learn their home language.

## Discussion point

Sri Lankan refugees, as well as those escaping other countries are often forced to pay 'agents' a lot of money to arrange forged passports, flights or smuggling refugees across borders. Agents may make large sums of money out of refugees, others very little. Some people argue that the activities of these agents is always wrong. Another point of view is that agents are helping desperate people.
**What do you think?**

CHAPTER SIX

# Looking to the Future

"I want to continue studying, I want to become an archaeologist."
**Fatma, from Kurdistan**

"I'll try and bring all my family here when I am 18."
**Kasim, from Somalia**

"I hope that the fighting stops soon and that everyone can have a normal life and that children get the chance to go to school." **Lakshmi, from Sri Lanka**

Ask any refugee what they dream of and they will say safety, peace and the chance to return home.

## Returning home

Almost all refugees wish to return home. For many refugees this dream will come true. Some refugees go back in small groups. Often just a family travel together. Other refugees return as part of an organised group. The UNHCR helps refugees return home. It provides returning refugees with transport, packs of material and sometimes money to help in the first months back home. The UNHCR and other organisations may provide seeds and tools so that returning farmers can plant new crops as soon as possible. Returning refugees may also carry home dried food like flour and lentils, to eat while waiting for new crops to grow.

### Refugees who have returned

| Group | Dates of Return | Numbers |
| --- | --- | --- |
| Mozambicans | 1992-1995 | 1,652,000 |
| Iraqis | 1991 | 1,510,000 |
| Rwandans | 1994- | 1,000,000 |
| Cambodians | 1992-1993 | 387,000 |
| Bosnians | 1996 | 600,000 |

# Resettling in another country

Returning home is not possible for some refugees. Wars can go on for many years, and a refugee's home country may not be safe enough. Land mines may prevent refugee farmers returning to their land. Or farms and homes may be occupied by newcomers, preventing refugees from returning. It is also important to help those refugees who can never return. They will need permanent homes, locally, or in another country. Language teaching and job training may also be provided to help refugees rebuild their lives. For those refugees like Kasim, who have been split up from their families, refugees may also need help tracing missing family members.

An Afghan refugee in Pakistan UNHCR

# The search for peace

All the young refugees whose stories are told in this book had hopes that fighting and human rights abuses would stop in their home countries. A world without war and injustice is the dream of all refugees. And everyone has a role to play in making this happen. The UN and governments may be involved in bringing about a ceasefire to a war, or writing a peace agreement. But ordinary people too are involved in making peace. We have a responsibility to ensure that other students are not bullied in school. We all have the responsibility to ensure that people are not treated differently because of their religion, beliefs or ethnic groups. We all have the responsibility to work for a peaceful world.

## The costs of conflict

One person in 130 alive today is a refugee or an internally displaced person.

There are presently 30 large scale wars being fought today. Most of these are civil wars between different groups of people living in the same country.

Since 1992 over five million children have died in wars.

Six million children have been disabled in wars since 1982.

Between 1969 and 1992 some 3,027 people were killed as a result of the violence in Northern Ireland.

In 1992 there were 130,000 racially motivated crimes recorded in the UK.

Source: Oxfam

# What you can do

Refugees depend on your support in many ways. Here are some ideas of things you can do.

Join a campaigning organisation that works to prevent people becoming refugees, or works to promote refugees' rights.

Get in touch with refugee organisations to collect more information about refugees.

Inform your friends about refugees by making a school display. You can use the information you have collected from refugee organisations. You might want to show the different aspects of refugees' lives throughout the world in the display. Find out why people become refugees and what help they need in a new country. You could put your display on a noticeboard in the school entrance or in a classroom.

Contact a refugee organisation to invite a refugee speaker to come and talk to your class. You could add what you learn from the speaker to your display.

Organise a fundraising event to collect money for a refugee organisation. You can organise a sponsored walk, football or swimming event to collect money. You will

A young volunteer at a day centre for refugees, London

need to plan your fundraising activity and get permission to organise your event. You will also have to design a sponsorship form. A fundraising event can also inform people about the needs of refugees!

Write to your local newspaper about your fundraising event. Explain why you are doing this, and what refugees need. You could also contact your local radio station.

Contact an organisation that works with refugees in your town or city. You can find out if they need children's clothes or toys and organise a school collection. Many refugee children arrive in a new country with very few belongings.

Algerian refugees in the UK

MAGGIE LAMBERT

Be a friend to a refugee in your school or neighbourhood. Make sure that refugee children who are new to your school know where to go for lessons and lunch. Your friendship can go a long way in helping a refugee adjust to life in a new country.

Remember refugees are ordinary people just like everyone else. It is just that their recent experiences have been difficult and dangerous. They need your support.

# Dictionary

**Civil war**  A war between two or more groups of people within one country.

**Deportation**  Being sent back home, or to live in another country against your will. Sometimes people who have fled to the UK are sent back home against their will.

**Ethnic minority**  A group of people who share a distinct culture, usually different from most of the population.

**Family tracing**  A search for a lost member of a family who may have become separated during a war. The Red Cross is the main international organisation that carries out family tracing.

**Guerrillas**  An armed group of people that organises small scale attacks.

**Internally displaced people** People who have been forced to flee their homes because of war or other dangers. Unlike refugees, they remain in their own country. There are no international human rights laws to protect them.

**Landmine** An explosive device placed in the ground and designed to explode when a person steps on it.

**Malnutrition** Illnesses caused by not having enough food or enough of the right food to eat.

**Non-governmental organisations** These are organisations that are not run by governments. The Refugee Council and refugee self-help groups are non-governmental organisations.

**Pressure group** An organisation that campaigns for its members, or for a particular cause, for example human rights. Amnesty International is a pressure group.

**Racism** When people are treated differently because they belong to a particular ethnic group. Racism can take many forms. People can be victims of violent attacks. They can also be treated differently by employers and school teachers.

**Refugees** The 1951 UN Convention Relating to the Status of Refugees defines refugees as people who have 'a well founded fear of persecution for reasons of race religion, nationality, membership of a particular social group or political opinion'. Some 131 countries have signed these international laws which lay down how countries should treat refugees.

**UN** The United Nations, an international organisation that works for peace. Sometimes the UN sends soldiers to regions of war. Almost all of the world's countries are members of the UN.

**UNHCR** The United Nations

Mozambican refugees given food rations for their return to their home villages          UNHCR

**Scapegoat** A person or a group of people who are blamed for a problem they have not directly caused. Today, in Europe, refugees are being blamed by some people for causing unemployment and housing shortages.

**Self-help group** A small organisation founded by a group of people to help themselves and others faced with the same problems. Refugee self-help groups are sometimes called refugee community organisations.

High Commissioner for Refugees. It is part of the UN and is the main international organisation that helps refugees. It sees that they do not face danger as well as organising the supply of food, water and shelter to refugee camps. UNHCR also works to find solutions for refugee movements.

**Unaccompanied refugee child** A child or young person under 18 who has lost their parents or usual carers or become separated from them.

# Further resources: books and videos

## For students

Filipovic, Z (1994) *Zlata's Diary*. Methuen. The diary of a girl growing up in war-torn Sarajevo.

King, J. (1992) *The Kurds*. Wayland

Laird, E (1991) *Kiss the Dust*. Heinemann. The story of a Kurdish girl forced to flee to London.

Minority Rights Group (1998) *Forging New Identities: Young Refugees and Minority Students Tell Their Stories*

Rady, M (1994) *The Breakup of Yugoslavia*. Wayland.

Refugee Council (1998) The *Deceiver*. A Somali folk story illustrated by Abdulkadir Muhamed Jama.

Rutter, J. (1994) *Jewish Migrations*. Wayland.

Serraillier, Ian (1956) *The Silver Sword*. Puffin. A fictional account of the flight of four young refugees.

Silverman, R. (1997) *A Bosnian Family*. Lerner Publications, Minneapolis.

Warner, R. (Ed) (1991) *Voices from Kurdistan and Voices from Somalia*. Minority Rights Group. Two collections of testimonies of refugee children.

Wilkes, S. (1994) *One Day We Had To Run*. Evans Brothers. Stories and paintings of refugee children from Ethiopia, Somalia and Sudan.

## For teachers

BBC Books (1995) *The Death of Yugoslavia*.

Oxfam (1997) *Making Peace: teaching about conflict and reconciliation*.

Refugee Council *The Sri Lanka Monitor*. A monthly journal about events in Sri Lanka.

Rutter, J. (1996) Refugees: *We Left Because We Had To*. A 240 page teaching resource for 14-18 year olds, containing testimonies, background information and activities. Available price £6 from the Refugee Council.

## Videos

*Refugee Children*. A 45 minute video of refugee children's testimonies.
Available from the Refugee Council.

*Refugee Voices*. A 25 minute video of young Bosnian, Kurdish, Somali and Vietnamese refugees telling their stories.
Available from Channel Four Schools on 01926-433333.

School students hand in a petition about the human rights of refugees to the House of Commons
EDMUND CLARK

# Organisations

**Amnesty International** - UK
99-119 Rosebery Avenue
London EC1R 4RE
0171-814-6200

A worldwide human rights
organisation. Amnesty
International produces a wide
range of published material and
is engaged in human rights
education.

**Anne Frank Educational
Trust**
PO Box 432
Bushey
Herts WD2 1QU

**Commission for Racial
Equality**
Elliot House
10 Allington Street
London SW1 5EH
0171-828-7022

**Development Education
Association**

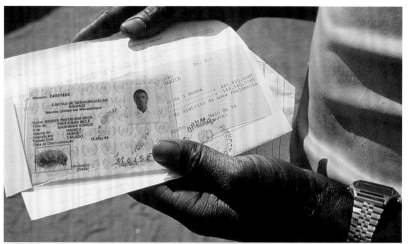

Identity documents of returning Mozambican refugee          UNHCR

3rd Floor
29-31 Cowper Street
London EC1R 4AP
0171-490-8108

**Irish Refugee Council**
Arran House
35 Arran Quay
Dublin 7

**Minority Rights Group**
379 Brixton Road
London SW9 7DE
0171-978-9498

**Oxfam**
274 Banbury Road
Oxford OX2 7DZ
01865-311311

**Refugee Council**
3 Bondway
London SW8 1SJ
0171-820-3000

The Refugee Council can put
you in touch with regional
refugee organisations and
refugee community
organisations. It also publishes a
wide range of educational
materials.

**Save the Children**
17 Grove Lane
London SE5 8RD
0171-703-5400

**UNHCR** (UK and Ireland)
21st Floor, Millbank Tower
21-24 Millbank
London SW1P 4QP
0171-828-9191

Vietnamese refugees          HOWARD DAVIES

51